POEMLESS NIGHTS

by

David Kamali

First edition, 2021

Cover illustration: iStock.com/Begash

Förlag: BoD – Books on Demand, Stockholm, Sverige

Tryck: BoD – Books on Demand, Norderstedt, Tyskland

ISBN: 978-91-8007-747-7

www.davidkamali.com

Dedicated to all who learned to love by loving.

Foreword

THE day after I published my first poetry collection, the leader of the church I was intending contacted me and told me that publishing my book was a mistake. He said that the book would affect people negatively and that "a Christian person doesn't write a book like this". I did not know what to say. I was shocked. I had prepared myself for critics but never thought my closest friends could be the first to criticise. My belief in God is an essential part of my life. I risked my life in Iran by following Jesus and becoming a Christian when I was 15. I was criticised then, and I was criticised now. After that conversation, I questioned myself and the choices I had made. I wanted to contact the publisher and ask them to cancel the contract, but there was this deep gentle voice inside my heart that reassured me that I had made the right choice. A month later, I was contacted by a woman from the United States. She explained that she came across the book and wanted to read only a few pages and ended up reading the whole collection. She mentioned that while reading the book, she cried because she found herself in the story. She thanked me and said that she found a stronger hope and a steadier faith after reading my book, and she encouraged me to continue. I was so humbled by her words. I could not sleep that night. I had to let the world know the untold part of the story of Dave and Soul, so I started to write. That was the start of *Poemless Nights*.

I met the leader of the church after that and wanted to clear things out.

"Do you want me here?" I asked him.

"You're not part of the church anymore. I don't want you to be here. End of discussion!" He said.

I put my hand on his shoulder, looked into his eyes, thanked him and walked away. I was excluded from the church, like an outcast. I knew I wasn't perfect, but I was working really hard to be better. I didn't know why this happened. I wanted to give up on everything; I was so tired. Then God reminded me of the story of the man with leprosy. Leprosy sufferers had to leave their homes, families, community, and everything else. They were excluded from the community, too. They were forbidden to have any contact with people who did not have leprosy since they were unclean. The man with leprosy in the Bible (Matthew 8) was poorly treated by the religious leaders and others, but in the midst of his depression and brokenness, Jesus came and "touched" him and made him "clean". I knew what I had to do. I trusted God and I kept moving forward, and that's why I chose to publish this poetry collection. I wanted to let others know that sometimes we may not know why some things happen, but it makes life more interesting. The important thing is to keep moving forward. Imagine that you wake up and know all the answers to all of your questions, then wouldn't life be boring the day after?

David Kamali
The Author

Contents

1 | Cast Away

years past.
I felt closely cast
away
when I left, and I give a thousand years
for a day
with her.

2 | The Old Road

one day I was driving
on the old road from work,
listening to a client
who impulsively spoke.

my eyes focused on the road
passing by the old bus stop.
I couldn't believe she was there,
the same woman I once loved.

stop! break! and turn back!
I couldn't believe it with my eyes.
"sorry sir, I will call you back.
it's emergency and no lies."

I turned the car and honked twice.
"jump in. I can give you a ride."
"what on earth you doing, Dave?
come and park the other side."

she jumped in, and I drove fast
like movies, like a police car.
her voice echoed in my ears

like perfect tones of a guitar.

"how are you, Dave? my old friend!"
honestly, we were more than friends!
"I'm good, Soul. long time no see."
her look had changed like fashion trends.

"it's been years since we last met.
I see you drive a fancy car.
you look different with that beard,
by the way, my place is not so far.

stop here! I live there!
thank you for the ride and your time.
let's keep in touch for old times' sake
I want to hear the hills you've climbed."

for old times' sake
"okay."
I called it fate.

3 | First Date, Again

I called her the following weekend.
the exact number
that I once wanted to reach
many times
but went straight to voicemail
was now ringing.

my life felt like a circle
I have been running it for 2pi.
now I was back at the same spot
my first date with her
again.
does it count as the first date, though?

4 | Ride It Safely

I told her to pack a bag,
a small one with some snack
and a windproof jacket.
"it might get windy."

next hour,
I had my brown leather jacket,
black gloves,
protective,
blue jeans and brown Suede shoes
when she saw me
on my motorbike
waiting for her
in front of her new apartment
still old, though.
she smiled.
"I love your bike, Dave,
but please
ride it safely."
"just jump on!"
she put her helmet on.
her long Afro
trespassed the helmet,

and landed on her back.
I wish I could just drive
and not look back.
there are moments in life
you want to hold on to
forever.
nothing lasts forever
in this life
except for memories
like those nights in Paris.

when I was a kid
my mom taught me not to play with fire
"it will burn you, son!"
yet she never told me
how many times she burned her soft hands
(not so soft anymore)
to keep us warm.
I could see it now,
vividly,
that I let the fire to visit me.
I had a fire in my heart.
was the fire keeping my temple warm
or was it burning it down?
it was worth it either way.
she was worth it either way.

5 | Home

one down,
four up,
ignoring the neutral
the same way life disregarded the neutrals.
fifth gear,
we were on the motorway
skipping the traffic.
I could hear an older man behind his wheel
cursing us.
I understood him though.
he wanted to get to his destination
but he couldn't,
obstacles on his way.
but I was reaching the destination
no obstacles on my way.
I called it jealousy.
I ignored it helplessly
like I ignored the smell of Hennessy
from the night before.

I felt the evening breeze
smuggling herself
into my helmet

sensing my skin.
she wanted me
but I was taken
by the moment.
a gentleman never cheats.

I felt her hands
tightening around my waist.
I felt her head,
leaning on my back.
I looked at the mirror.
I saw her hair
racing the wild wavy wind,
like a kite
in the hands of a child.
don't let go!
I felt like a knight
on his black Shire
lifting the hands of his lover
taking her to their new home.

home,
I want to take her
home,
maybe a weekend in
Rome.

6|Dancing Days

we sat down near the fire.
the coals were beating their friends,
the firewood,
to give life to the fire.
the woods
cried
due to the beating
and the burning,
but they didn't move.
they should have.
a revolution
starts only with a movement.
maybe they wanted to
but they feared they would be ruthlessly suppressed
by the fire
like the people of Iran.
they had accepted their destiny
to burn,
to drain,
to light,
to heat,
and to become ashes.
the coals

said nothing.
they just burned,
and burned,
and burned.
they reminded me of people.

the marshmallows on the heat
turned brown and black.
"it's hot."
"chew it fast!"
she laughed.
I felt like the moon was close,
more prominent than usual.
I thought for a second
I was dreaming.
I did pray for this moment
but didn't think
God would allow it to happen.
He works in mysterious ways.

I could hear the laughter of some campers,
they were happy.
I could listen to the movement of the river
down the valley.
where was he going?
was he in search of his destiny
the ocean
or was he just running
and running
until there was no place to run?

I could hear the birds
whispering in an unknown language,

they probably gossiped about us.
maybe they said to each other:
"this guy is an idiot
to fall in love
with the same woman
who robbed him of his heart."
or maybe they said:
"we understand you, Dave.
you'll never know
if it is
the net of the hunter
or the food from the ranger
until you try.
yet, the risk is high!"

I could hear the crickets
chirping.
it felt like they were blowing whistles,
whistleblowers.
I wish I could blow the whistle on love,
and tell the world
that if we don't give love time,
we will have no time to love.

I could see the fireflies
attracting mates,
and preys,
and my eyes,
and her attention,
with their cold light,
green,
pistachio.
"they are dancing."

her comment made sense.
they were dancing
with the jazz of the forest
under the light of the moon.
"do you want to join them?"
"nah, I'm good. my dancing days are behind."
"nobody is ever too old for a dance."

7 | Unforgettable Smile

she hugged me.
her hugs felt like a woman
who hugged his man
after he came back from war,
safe,
grown,
mature,
secure.
she looked into my eyes,
those coyote eyes,
dark, bright.
she kissed my cheek.
somehow
she knew
I wasn't ready to let her in
in my heart,
again.
she surrendered the helmet
with her fears trapped in it.
motorcyclophobia.

she went to her door,
and smiled.

that unforgettable smile.
she turned her key
and disappeared in three.
no words were spoken.
she probably thought
that I still hated goodbyes.
she didn't know
after she left
I started to embrace goodbyes.
I realised a long time ago
that some people come to our lives
to stay,
and some are just there
to teach us
how to let go.
I embraced goodbyes.

8 | Words of Your Heart

I couldn't sleep that night.
it's scary being on the height
not knowing what is down there.
emptiness,
fullness,
vagueness,
wholeness.
sometimes,
try to stress
less!
close your eyes,
open your ears,
hear the words of your heart,
the gentle voice from deep within,
and take a leap of faith!

9 | A Leap of Faith

I called the next day,
took a leap of faith, no doubt,
and I asked her out.

10 | Harbour

we met each other
near the harbour.
two ships in the distance,
loading dock.
two birds in the sky,
goose and duck.

I put my hand on her leg,
tenderly,
fondling her beautiful soul.
she held my arm with her hand.
I was nervous.
it had been years
since I was so careless.

she was like a robber
who came to my house,
twice,
to rob the treasure of my heart.
I let her in.
Stockholm syndrome.

there were three men,

testing their luck to
catch a fish.
there were three fish,
pushing their luck to
eat a good meal,
served to them with a purpose.

there was a woman,
running.
maybe from destiny
maybe for training.

"why are you always so observant, Dave?"
"I like to see the world in detail."
"why?"
"I don't know,
but I believe God created these details
in everything,
in us,
to teach us something."
"like what?"
"like small details
can make great impacts."

II | Her Melanin, Her Skin

a long walk near the ocean.
mother beach smuggled some of her children,
the sand grains,
into my boots.
they were in search of happiness,
in another part of town.
maybe a new start,
or perhaps an old ending.
I felt sorry for her,
she was stepped on,
many times,
by men she did not even know.

she was focused.
the sunset painted the nature of nature,
nature painted the people,
and people polluted both of them.
there was a dog
who had claimed a wooden stick
as his precious prize.
I could feel the rise
of the water,
and she was getting hotter

in my eyes.
I remembered
the taste of her lips
the madness of her eyes
and the beauty of her skin.

Her Melanin,
Her Skin.

I could see a woman diving into the water.
splash!
I could hear the cry of a child after falling.
scratch.

I could hear the joyful shout of a young man
from the volleyball court
who just scored.
they were playing
3 by 3.
their feet
made monuments
on the sand.
the white-yellow-blue ball
seemed tired
of the slaps
on her cheeks
by adult men
and their hands.
but she couldn't talk
could she?
even though she would
her voice would've not been heard.
so unfortunate.

we sat on a bench
hand in hand.
I could feel the sweat of her hands
she was nervous.
I knew her,
deeply.
maybe even more than myself.
she knew me,
keenly.
maybe even more than myself.
"what are you thinking about, Soul?"
"I'm not thinking,
I'm reflecting."
she said
and leaned back.
her head on my shoulder,
my heart grew bolder.
I think I still love you,
your soul and your value.
the sun looked at her watch,
she knew her time had come to an end.
she thought about how all endings are sad,
even the happy endings.
we watched the sunset to the end,
just me and her
without an exchange of words.
sometimes,
our hearts speak enough.

12 | Exotic

Netflix was on,
I wasn't concerned.
she was my concern.
her lips made me high,
exotic.
"Dave,
wait!"
I stopped,
immediately.
"what's wrong, Soul?"
"do you still love me, Dave?
"I don't know. I once did."
"I know when I left
you were hurt.
but I'm back
on track
with my life."
"give my heart
some time.
I will find
the same love
again."

she smiled,
enthusiastically.
"you know Dave,
you are the first person who does that."
"does what?"
"you stopped
when I said stop!"
"a real man takes a no
as a no. Simple."
"I respect you, Dave.
you're an honest man."
"I do the best I can,
to be a better man."
she kissed me again.

13 | Falling Apart

sometimes,
falling apart
is what brings us back together.

14 | Dangerous

I got high
on her cologne.
I didn't like to be alone.
I was the king in her throne.
Mary Josephine and Al Capone.
bad energy stay out of my zone!
dangerous,
we were together again.
dangerous,
we didn't follow the brain.
dangerous,
our hearts were to blame.
dangerous,
she stayed because of the rain.
dangerous.

15 | Imperfections

I woke up by the sound of boiling water
she was making coffee.
"I love your apartment, Dave.
you live like a prince."
"prince? please!
I'm still the same goofy guy."
"the imperfect one?"
"exactly!"
she smiled.
"I'm not looking for perfection anymore,
I prefer wholeness,"
her word calmed my heart,
and made beauty of this whole mess.
"you know Dave,
accepting your imperfections
is the first sign of perfection."

16 | Notebook

after breakfast
she went to my office room.
she observed it closely.
a big desk with an iMac,
a black office chair,
a big library of books
in the background,
a box of cigars,
cedarwood.
handmade cigars,
the smell of Cuba,
with a taste of Communism.
so that's why I spat
every time I smoked.
a Chacom pipe,
marble glossy cover,
made in France.
It's true what they say:
"France changes people."

"why do you smoke that wooden pipe?"
she said, smiling.
"well, it makes me smarter."

"how is that possible?"
"when I smoke, I shut my mouth
and it hinders me from talking.
instead, I listen."

on my desk
she found a notebook
that contained some poems.
"can you read them for me?"
"are you sure?"
"I am. I miss your poems."
"okay then."
so I started to read:

17 | A Path

"

everyone has a story,
listen to it carefully.
everyone has a path,
observe it watchfully.
everyone has flaws,
ignore them, mindfully.
everyone has a destiny,
honour it, rightfully.

18 | The Road

I will stop
only if I give up,
not when the road is finished.

19 | No Doubts

loneliness
is the only time
you have no doubts.

20 | No Love

when my dad left
I was less than one.
I was a mess and none
to him.
it was me, mom,
and a big bro, Tom.

mom worked hard,
Daily.
she came home
lately.
her face,
palely.
dinner was not ready
most of the time.
I knew it would lead
to a life of crime.
no love,
no love,
no tengo amor.

21 | Ocean

I was filled
with emptiness,
but I won
my failures.
I asked myself:
"who bounded
the boundaries?
who washed
the ocean?
who broke
the broken?
who captured
the freedom?
who blew
the winds away?"

22 | Gentleman

wisdom, courage, compassion,
a simple heart with passion,
are the traits of a gentleman.
these are shown by his actions.
"

23 | Pure

"wow, Dave.
I am shocked.
these poems are now locked
inside my heart.
you are a
pure, proud, powerful poet.
you have a
secure, segmented, safe sound.
you are a
great, goofy, gorgeous guy.
you have a
mild, meek, moody mind."
"see! you can be
a poet too, Soul."
"maybe I'll reach that goal."

we both laughed.
time passed
fast.

24 | Misspelled

she opened my drawer.
still the same curious girl.
inside was a book,
the enemy of the fool.
newly written
with the title: "A Poerty Collection"
"did you write this?"
"yes. It will be published soon."
she laughed.
"Dave! You misspelled poetry.
it's P-O-E-T-R-Y."
she saw my
smile.
"you are right,
but that's perfect poetry.
mine is imperfect.
just like its spelling,
just like myself."

she took my pen,
and wrote something.
"read it later!"
she said.

then we left
my place.

I opened the book
as soon as I came back.
it was written:
"perfection is not a necessity.
I still love you!
yours truly,
the imperfect Suol"

Suol,
S-U-O-L
misspelled.
like imperfect poetry
P-O-E-R-T-Y.

25 | Well Dressed

Saturday night,
outside.
lukewarm cold,
lukewarm warm.
those gorgeous eyes
read my thoughts.
that seductive black skin
seduced me.
those desirable lips
desired me.
I wanted her so badly.
pedestrian walking, looking, talking.
I didn't care.
I wanted her
for life.

is it wrong to love?
or is it love to wrong?
I would never wrong you, Soul!
my destiny on a scroll.

her hands were sweating,
stressed.

she didn't know I was
blessed
to have her. She was well
dressed.

that beautiful dark blue dress.
her hair was covered
in a black headwrap.
her golden earrings
shone like diamonds.
I could see her pride.
I could feel her power.
I could sense her presence.
I could hear her thoughts.
we walked through the park,
she stood up near the high trees
the moon was over her head.
she had her arms crossed.
she walked,
slowly,
smoothly.
she looked up.
her lips were moving.
was she talking to God
or was she singing with the moon?
I watched her.
I loved her,
again.

26 | How Love Works

"Dave,
why me?
you literally
have infinitely
options!"
"is there an answer to this question?
because I don't know how love works.
I just accept you as who you are,
the rest is my heart's work."
she smiled.
I loved how I made her happy.

27 | The Same Ring

she didn't know
I still kept the same ring I bought for her
years ago.

28 | Different

"Dave,
what do you want in life?
happiness?"
"I'm already the happiest!"
"peace of mind?"
"I've found the best peace of mind
in life you can find."
"then what? maybe a meaning?"
"you know I have a purpose,
but I also found a meaning
this evening
with you."
"so what do you want?"
"I want to wake up
beside the woman I love
every day.
look! I had my sins
washed away.
I want to age
both in life
and in spirit
with the woman I love
and the strength I inherit.

I want to have a family,
children
many,
a dog
maybe.
I want us to build a house
I want us to calm the chaos.
I want her to hold my hand
at nights when we pray.
I want to hold her hand
when we watch our children play.
I want her to hold my hand
in the morning when we worship.
I want to hold her hand
in times of hardship.
I want her to be on my side
when I say goodbye
at the end of this journey
cause the afterlife doesn't scare me.
we have God
on our side."

I saw the tears break the chains of her eyes
was it sad tears
or happy ones?
she came close
she touched my face
I saw my reflection
in her eyes.
I didn't notice my own tears
I wanted to hold her
for a thousand years.
"Dave,

you're just
different."

29 | Bar

we sat outside the bar,
she drank her mojito
from the short black straw.
the glass in her hands
gave her dark skin
a new texture.
her lips kissed the straw
and made me jealous.
her eyes caught my eyes
"stop staring!"
she smiled,
still drinking.
I saw her classiness,
she saw my classicness.
a glass of whiskey,
with a taste of honey,
old school.
the two ice cubes
in my glass
melted in their destiny.

what was she thinking
when she smiled?

about the past
or the future,
or just the moment?
some questions in life
are never answered.

I lighted up a cigar,
Cohiba short.
"that will kill you one day,"
she said, rolling her eyes.
her perfect beautiful gorgeous eyes.
"think about the length of your life!"
"I'm more concerned about the depth of my life."
I said with a silly grin,
but for her sake,
I put down the cigar.

the cigar died within minutes.
his purpose was not fulfilled.
he was chosen
to be smoked.
his failure
was because he stopped
pursuing his purpose.
he quitted.
the match wanted to tell him:
"rest,
but never quit!"
but he feared
that the cigar's revival
may cost him his life.
he kept his silence like many people.

30 | Dance Floor

she took my hand
and ran
to the dance floor.
it was her jam.
my hand guided her waist,
her waist guided my hands.
her hands locked my emotions,
she rested her head on my chest
it's good to be tall.

the dance floor
froze.
people
froze.
time
froze.

it was me and her
and the sound of music.
a holy moment.

31 | The Night Was Young

after the dance
she went to the bartender
to order her second mojito.
I didn't know why
she never let me pay for her drinks.
was it a sign of respect
or independence?
I declined her proposal
for another drink.
a man has his limits.
I went outside
and sat down,
waiting for her.
the night was young.

32 | Time Froze

I went back to the bar.
I remembered
she had forgotten
her bag in the car.

I heard her
telling another guy:
"you have no right
to touch my body!"
loudly,
proudly.
I rushed in
"what's going on, love?"
"this guy just came out of nowhere
and grabbed my waist."
"none of your business,
mate.
her beauty shall be shared."
the guy said.
HOW DARE YOU!
time froze again.
I don't know if it was
the smell of alcohol

or his words
that disgusted me
the most.
maybe both.
I looked at Soul,
she was on the verge of tears.
I haven't seen that in years.
I looked at my hands
these God-given tools of love
now became weapons of mass destruction.
my knuckles
broke that guy's nose.
one punch was required.

time reset again.
two guards held my hands
from behind.
the guy
was having a deep sleep
with a broken nose
on the dance floor.

33 | Cell

I sat in a cell
until further notice.
a cell
2 by 3 or 3 by 4
yellow mildish vague floor.
a bed and a chair,
grey colour,
irony.
the cell added to my loneliness.
what an irony!

I wondered in that cell,
who is truly free?
a free mind behind bars
or a closed mind outside the bars.

I wondered in that cell
if the prison guards
are also prisoners
with the prisoners
as their prison guards.

I felt in that cell

like a workless worker
like a fatherless father
like a guardless guard
like a helpless helper
like a thoughtless thought
of a characterless character
with a speechless speech
at an endless end
with a heartless heart
and a painless pain.
indeed I felt in that cell
like a poemless poet
surviving his poemless nights.

push-ups,
sit-ups,
shadowboxing,
anything to take my mind away
from these closed walls.
time moved slowly in a cell.
each minute
felt like an hour.
I was there for many hours.
the guard brought me a cup of water
cold
two Ice cubes,
what an irony!
"why did you do it?"
"to defend her honour.
he needed to know
that a sexy dress
doesn't mean yes."
"is she your wife?"

"no. Just a woman I once loved."
"I'm finishing my shift soon.
do you need anything else?"
"thanks.
just a question.
what would you do
if you were in my shoes?"
he looked at his brass ring.
married,
a couple of years, probably.
he kept his silence.
his silence echoed in my cell.
"I understand if you don't want to answer.
it is known everywhere
en svensk tiger!
(a Swede keeps silent)
but you shouldn't.
speak your truth
no matter the cost!
it may put you in prison
but it will set you free,
and that's how you're created to be."
"honestly, you are right.
I don't know,
what I would do
if I were you."
he left and came back again.
"you're free to go!"

34 | Police Station

outside the police station,
she was waiting for me.

I could notice she was worried
sick.
I could catch her heartbeat,
weak.
I could feel her thoughts,
meek.
I could hear her silence
speak.
I could see the red blush on her
cheek.
I could read her toughness,
Greek.
I could see the moon in her eyes,
unique.
I could climb her body with my hands, mountain
peak.
I could hear the unspoken words
leak.
I could desire those closed lips,
beak.

I could sense her difficulties,
eke!

I could, but I chose
to go
to her.
I held her,
she held me.
eternity
seemed a certainty.

"don't ever do that again!"

she tried
to hide
her tied
eyes
but put her pride
aside
and cried
from outside
and inside
until her eyes
were dried.

35 | Time

time passed.
our intimacy developed,
slow but vast.

36 | Amir

I sat on the floor.
hands crossed,
head between my knees,
painful.
I listened to Jeremy's voicemail
again.

"Dave!
Amir was shot yesterday
while he was on his way
home from training.
two bullets,
one reached his heart.
painless death.
the police said
it was a robbery,
he was in the wrong place.
his family has invited us
for the funeral.
it's such a shame, man.
he was a good guy.
don't forget to buy
flowers!

see you tomorrow.
don't drink in your sorrow!
love you, bro.
you'll get through."

how can death be painless
for someone who doesn't believe
in the afterlife?
I cried.

Soul entered the apartment
using the spare key.
she ran to me.
"let me be!"
she hugged me
"can't you see?
he is gone.
I am done
with this country
and its system.
they say
the shooter
was newly released
from prison.
penalty reduced.
this country
always talks about rights
but never about obligations.
weren't they obligated
to keep the shooter in jail?"

she kissed me.
no hesitation.

no spoken words.
she heard my pain
and listened,
carefully,
respectfully,
tearfully.

37 | The Urge

I asked her
to leave.
"believe
me
I want you
but you see
I need to be
alone."
she left.
I felt
the urge
to write,
to fight
the pain
that night.

so I wrote:

38 | Rich Heart

"

don't judge this rich heart of mine
I came from under the line
of poverty.
nothing bothers me
anymore.
they said it was a robbery
and made a mockery
of it.
come and see these watery
eyes!
I'm sad
but not surprised.
damn the big lies
of that unwise
politician
who ties Amir's death
to an accident
and denies
to revise
his politics
and instead invites
the same criminals

who shot Amir
for some pizza
and fries.
his action defies
the democracy
in society.
please stop
and do your job
properly!

39 | Offspring

the field of my hopes was
dried, empty, unworthy
like the words of a politician
who chose his comfort
over the destiny of millions.
there was only one tree left
in the field of my hopes.
the old tree feared the axe of the lumberjack
less he knew
the handle of the axe
that cut him deep
was the offspring of his own.
wooden.
the old tree told the axe:
"I can hear the sound of your wooden hand
and your steely heart.
don't worry!
cut! cut deeply!
it is your destiny to cut.
my destiny is to grow again."

40 | Poemless Nights

my poems became the voice of the broken,
the voice of the unheard,
the voice of the unknown.

they became the voice of a teacher
who was suppressed by others
because of his political ideology.
last I heard
he was fired,
his certificate was revoked.

they became the voice of a believer
of Jesus Christ
in the Islamic Republic of Iran
(not republic at all).
last I heard
she was sentenced to death
by hanging.

they became the voice of a woman
in a society where the boys
learned to respect men
and look down on a woman

even though they came from a woman.
last I heard
she was stoned to death.

they became the voice of the writer
who warned people
about the danger of
Socialism,
the danger of the Left,
the danger that is left.
last I heard
he disappeared mysteriously,
never to be found.

they became the voice of a journalist
who identified the leader of a gang.
last I heard
he was found dead
in his car
with his pregnant wife
shot dead.
dead shot.

they became the voice of an immigrant
who immigrated for his values
only to be dis-valued and censored
in a neutral society.
last I heard
he was driving a cab
struggling to survive.

they became the voice of a man
who worked hard day and night

only to pay high taxes
for the safety of society.
(as the politicians put it!)
last I heard
he found out that his son
was knifed to death
by the mob
that controlled the area.

they became the voice of a police officer
who feared the process.
he knew that any criminal he caught
would be released from prison
due to technicality.
last I heard
he was threatened
after his colleague was shot.
so he gave up his job
and found a safer one.

they became the voice of a sick man
who registered
on the waiting list
of a hospital
where his taxes went to.
last I heard
he died of illness
but never saw a doctor.

they became the voice of the poet
who chose to write his truth
knowing that one day
he may be judged by it.

last I heard
he was cancelled
a victim of cancel culture.

my poems became
the voice of a poet
whose nights were without poems.
Poemless Nights.

41 | Bitter

I feel the bitterness and hate,
heavier than usual,
heavier than the colour of Scotch,
heavier than the eyes of a young soldier on the watch,
thinking about the woman he loves.
bitter.
heavier than the shadow of the same woman
who is forced to cover her hair.
heavier than the pain she carries
when she is forced into a marriage.
bitter.
heavier than the orders of a man
who is now the legal partner of the woman.
heavier than the hands of the man
on the beautiful face of the same woman.
bitter.
heavier than the silent cries of the woman
and the loud laughter of the man.
heavier than the hurtful words of the man
about the alluring body of the same woman.
bitter.
heavier than the emptiness of the soul of the woman
after the unsuccessful tries for a divorce.

heavier than the gossips about the same woman
by the close members of the family of the man.
bitter.
heavier than the disappointing looks of the father of the woman
who is also the business partner of the man.
heavier than the indifferent look of the same woman
forced into bed for the pleasure of the man.
bitter.
heavier than the depression of the woman
surrounded by the negative voice of the man.
heavier than the womb of the same woman
unwanted pregnancy for her but wanted for the man.
bitter.
heavier than the vomits of the woman
and the indifferent looks of the man.
heavier than the pills swallowed by the same woman
in the absence of the man.
bitter.
heavier than the news of the suicide of the same woman
and the search for a new mate by the man.
bitter.

42 | Who Am I

who am I?
I'm the voice of your gun,
I can be heard in the distant darkness.
I'm the fear inside the heart of the female officer
in a patriarchal society.
democracy on paper,
demagoguery in reality.
I'm the shaking hands on your open wound
that purifies the infections of your mind,
giving you false hope.
I know it pains.
I'm the empty bottle of an alcoholic,
the alcoholic who chose to drink his pain away
only to cause more pain.
I'm the painkiller sold by that drug dealer
who works at night
protection a zip code
he doesn't even owe.
I'm the small chosen words of a newspaper
that talks about the danger of criminality
and is censored directly.
I'm the lies of the Swedish politician
who says to the press:

"the risk of innocent people
being affected by criminality is little."
I'm the needles in the hands of that grandmother
whose fingers dance with the yarn
only to give birth to a sweater.
she knitted it for her grandson
not knowing
he was shot by a bullet
last night
in the same zip code.
he was looking to buy some painkillers
because he found his bottle empty
and got shot by the drug dealer
who sold those painkillers.
he had mistaken him for a rival.
the neighbours had heard the shot
and called the police
only to see the officer showed up late
because of her fear of the neighbourhood.
when she arrived, nothing could be done
except to hold her shaky hands
on his open wounds.
his death was mentioned in a small newspaper
but censored by the lies of the politician
in a society that cared less about obligations,
a society where the churches
feared people
more than they feared God.
a society
where these mistakes are repeated.
multiple mistakes
are not considered mistakes,
they are counted as habits.

bad habits.

my poems are those mistakes,
and my poemless nights,
a product of those mistakes.

43 | Dear God

dear God,
why does everyone have a broken side?
"

44 | Calvary

I told God:
"Father,
show me, and I will believe in you."
God whispered in my ear:
"my son,
believe in me, and I will show you."
"why don't you remove all the bad people, God?"
"removing the useless weeds
will uproot the good harvest.
I know losing a friend is the hardest."
"I wish I was like you, flawless."
"I still love you, regardless."

I realised that moment
the journey of finding your true self
always leads to a hill
called Calvary.

45 | Far Away

days past.
Soul and I didn't talk much.
and as one can foretell,
we were far away.

46 | Ivory Coast

I called her
and apologised
some days later.
I knew
I needed some times
to reflect.
she forgave me,
easily.
"can we meet tonight?"
"sorry, Dave.
I'm travelling tomorrow
to my homeland,
Ivory Coast."
"oh, sorry I didn't know."
"it's okay. It just happened.
I'm visiting my family,
will be back in nine weeks."
"I'm going to miss you."
"I know you will.
don't worry.
I promise I'll call
every night."
"okay, my lovely queen.

can you do me a favour
and bring me a bag of coffee bean?"
"of course.
the best you've ever seen."
"did you know, Soul,
when I was a kid
I thought Ivory Coast
was a coast
made of ivory."
she laughed,
her laughs were morphine
to my body.
"really?
Dave, you're so silly.
listen! I have to go to the store,
I'll talk to you soon mon amour."

47 | Long Flight

she texted me the first night:
"I arrived!
long flight,
I want to talk but I'm really sleepy.
though I wish you could've joined me tonight,
here in my hotel room.
me and you
we would've let our love resume."

she called me on her second night.
8 p.m. there,
10 p.m. here.
when we were separated
time was separated too.
she was excited.
she had met her family,
it was in a way
her source of sanity.
she said how much she missed me
and asked me if I remembered
the first time she kissed me.

I remembered clearly

that cold February night.

"I will be
at my distant cousin's village
that I had only seen in an old image,
so I might be busy
with the family.
but I'll call you when I can!"
"yes ma'am."
"kisses."

third day
no message.
forth day
no message.
fifth day
no message.
at night,
I called her.
no answer.
again,
no answer.
two text messages:
"hey beautiful, how are you?
call me when you can!"
no answer.
I tried everything,
every night,
no answer.
time passed quick,
and I was worried sick.
no answer.

48 | A Text

five weeks later,
a text.
"Dave,
I'm coming home
tomorrow.
pick me up at the airport,
8 p.m."
"Soul,
I've been worried.
my queen,
where have you been?
what have you seen?"

"just come!"

49 | Just Drive

I met her at the airport,
our conversation was short.
briefly finished.
"hi Soul,
I've missed you!"
"just drive home!"
"are you okay?"
"I'm alive.
please,
just drive!"

I drove her home.
she closed the car's door
and ran in.
I picked up her bags
and went upstairs.

Knock-Knock

no answer.
"Soul,
I'm coming in.
is that okay?"

a whisper:
"just put the bags inside
and leave!"

I went in.
I saw her pale face.
she was scared,
like an innocent woman on trail,
murder case.

"Soul,
what's wrong?
please,
talk to me!
I beg you!"

50 | Keep Calm

"Dave,
I'm pregnant!"
she fell on her knees,
crying.
I was shocked,
mouth closed,
paralysed.
"what do you mean?
we haven't had ..."
"it's not yours!"
she cried bitterly.

the world seemed to end
the moment she spoke.
I couldn't believe it.
keep calm!
keep calm!

"I don't understand,
whose is it?"
"nobody!"
"TELL ME!"
"MY UNCLE."

the world seemed to end
for her as well.
she didn't have much to say.
she didn't need to.
I knew the story,
you know it too.

"Soul...
did you
talk to the police?"
"the police?
are you serious?
is that so unclear
or mysterious
that they don't care!
this is normal,
it is a man's world.
nothing to be told!"

I paused,
quite quiet.
coordinating my thoughts.
words didn't come out,
tears did.
I cried,
she cried,
God cried.
the world laughed.

51 | Her Choice

"take me
by my hand, love!
I will take care of the baby
together with you."
she looked back,
and pushed my hand away.
"go away!
I want you to be free
without me.
I've made my choice,
go away!"

so I did.
I don't know if it was a mistake,
or it was for her sake,
but I left,
since I heard
her voice
and respected her choice.

52 | Last I Heard

last time I heard of her
she had moved to another city.
she had a son,
his name was Solomon.
we chose that name together
years ago
on our way to Copenhagen.
she was married.
arrange marriage.
by force or by choice
I do not know.
my heart broke
and was buried.
I walked away.

I try never to look back
for the sake of the love I lack.

**The End
Or Maybe
A New Beginning.**

Afterword

SOMETIMES things happen in our lives, and we do not understand why they happened, like the story of Dave and Soul. We may spend our whole life trying to understand the reasons behind them, but some questions are never meant to be answered. Maybe they happened to tear us down so we may build up ourselves again. Stronger. Renewed. To build a new and better house, the builder must tear down the old house first. Maybe they happened to bring us closer to those who experienced the same things because we will have empathy instead of sympathy. It is easier to walk in someone's shoes when they fit your feet. Maybe they happened to build our characters and make us stronger. A blacksmith needs to put the iron into a burning fire first in order to shape it into a sharp sword. Maybe they happened to help us to mature, to grow, and to develop. A seed needs to be buried first in order to produce good fruit. I spent days wondering why all these things happened, and to this day, I do not know why. Maybe some questions in life are better to be left alone, without an answer. Perhaps one day, my story connects to your story, and together, they make a better one. Just keep trusting God, and let Him guide your steps. He will never let your hand go.

In short, it has been an amazing process to write this poetry collection, and I hope that it has been pleasant to read. Acknowledgement must be made to those without whom this book would have never been completed. I genuinely hope that my story has touched your ardent heart.

Sincerely,
David Kamali
2021